This book is presented to:

_____

From:

_____

Date:

_____

BIG BAD BIBLE
BULLIES

BY SCOTT HAGAN
ILLUSTRATED BY DOUG HORNE

Charisma
KIDS
A STRANG COMPANY

Big Bad Bible Bullies
by Scott Hagan

Requests for information may be addressed to:

The children's book imprint of Strang Communications Company
600 Rinehart Rd., Lake Mary, FL 32746
www.charismakids.com

Children's Editor: Gwen Ellis
Copyeditor: Jevon Oakman Bolden
Design Director: Mark Poulalion
Designed by Joe De Leon

Library of Congress Control Number: 2004107758
International Standard Book Number: 1-59185-604-3

05 06 07 08 / LP / 5 4 3 2 1
Printed in China

Some Things You Need to Know

What Is a Bully?

A bully is anyone who picks on you, is mean to you, and makes you feel afraid.

What Might a Bully Do?

- A bully might hit, push, or threaten to do something to you.

- A bully might steal or break things that belong to you.

- A bully might call you names to insult you.

- A bully might lie or gossip about you to keep friends away.

- A bully might try to make you do things you don't want to do.

Bullies have been around since Bible times. Let's read their stories and see what happened to these people who acted mean.

CHAPTER 1
Sometimes You Need to Tell Someone

The Story of Esther and Haman

From the Book of Esther

Queen Esther of Persia was one of the most beautiful girls in the world. She was a Jew and so was her cousin Mordecai.

In Persia there lived a mean bully named Haman. He hated the Jews. One day he talked to the king about getting rid of the Jews. Esther and Mordecai were afraid when they heard what Haman had said.

Queen Esther wanted to save her people. Mordecai said, "Ask the king for help." Esther knew he was right. So she told the king everything Haman was planning to do. The king was angry. He punished Haman, and the Jewish people were saved.

You are not a coward if you ask for help.
Esther asked the king for help. The minute a
bully shows up tell a parent or teacher. They
are in your life to protect you. They can stop
the bully before he hurts you or other children.

CHAPTER 2
Sometimes You Must Have Courage

The Story of David and Goliath

From the First Book of Samuel, Chapter 17

The most famous bully in the Bible was the giant Goliath. He was nine feet tall with huge muscles and very bad breath. His main job was to scare God's people. Goliath and the Philistine army came out on one side of a valley. The army of Israel came out on the other side of the valley.

For forty days, Goliath screamed across the valley at God's army. He yelled, "I dare you to send a man to fight me." Nobody wanted to fight Goliath.

Bullies like to laugh at people or try to scare them. They pick on kids who are afraid of them. Sometimes bullies keep on being bullies because no one stops them.

God's people were scared. They didn't think anyone could stop Goliath. But God had a plan. A young boy named David brought food to his brothers. He heard Goliath yelling. He saw that everyone was afraid.

David prayed and asked God to help him. God filled his heart with courage. God showed him what to do. David called to Goliath, "You come after me with a sword and a spear, but I stand before you in the name of the Lord." Then David put a rock in his sling and flung it at Goliath. It hit Goliath in the head, and the giant died.

David found out that God is bigger than bullies—even nine-foot tall bullies with very bad breath.

CHAPTER 3
Sometimes You Need Your Friends' Help

The Story of Nehemiah and Sanballat

From the Book of Nehemiah, Chapters 2–6

Nehemiah was sad because the walls of Jerusalem were broken. God told him to rebuild the walls so that his hometown would be safe.

Nehemiah told his people, "We are helpless without strong walls. Let's work together to rebuild them."

Near Jerusalem lived a mean bully named Sanballat. He did not want the walls to be fixed. He tried every mean trick he could think of to stop Nehemiah. He called Nehemiah stupid. He said Nehemiah didn't know how to rebuild the walls.

Bullies try to hurt your feelings by calling you names. If that doesn't work, a bully might push you to scare you—especially if you are alone. Nehemiah didn't like being called stupid, but he went right on rebuilding the walls.

Then Sanballat asked his mean friend Tobiah to make fun of Nehemiah, too. So in front of all the people, Tobiah said that Nehemiah didn't have enough brains or muscles to rebuild the walls. Then they sent a messenger with a letter to scare Nehemiah. But he just prayed and went on working.

Nehemiah and his friends finished the walls in fifty-two days. Nehemiah won! God won!

When Sanballat saw that the walls were fixed, he gave up and went home.

Bullies like to pick on just one person. So when friends stick together, the bully gets scared. Friends who stick together and trust in God can do great things. They can even make bullies disappear.

CHAPTER 4
Sometimes a Bully Needs a Friend

The Story of Ananias and Saul

From the Book of Acts, Chapter 9

When Saul was a little boy, he learned about God. But as he grew up, he started hanging around with bullies who thought it was cool to be mean to people who loved Jesus. Saul became a very mean bully.

One day when he was out on bully business, Jesus stopped him and made him blind. Saul was scared. He had met someone more powerful than himself.

Blind Saul had to sit in a house and wait and think.

"I want you to go pray for Saul," the Lord told a man named Ananias.

Ananias didn't think this was a good idea at all. He knew Saul was mean. He knew Saul could hurt him. But the Lord knew that Saul needed a special friend like Ananias.

Finally Ananias obeyed God and found poor, blind Saul. Ananias put his hands on Saul and prayed for him. Suddenly Saul could see again! But even more wonderful was that God changed Saul's heart. Instead of being a bully, Saul began to help people learn about God's love.

God loves to smile! He smiles biggest when people's hearts change. Saul's heart changed, and God gave him a new name—Paul. Paul would not be a bully anymore.

If God can change bully Saul into loving Paul, maybe He can change the person who bullies you, too. Ask God to help you be a friend to that mean bully. Maybe, instead of "bully," his name will become "buddy."

CHAPTER 5
Sometimes You Need to Run Away

The Story of Joseph and Potiphar's Wife

From the Book of Genesis, Chapter 39

Joseph worked for an Egyptian officer named Potiphar. Potiphar put Joseph in charge of everything he owned. Potiphar's wife wasn't big and strong, but she was a bully anyway.

One day she tried to get Joseph to do something bad. Joseph said no. He kept on saying no, but she wouldn't leave him alone. So Joseph ran away. Fast!

Running away might feel like the bully is winning, but sometimes a bully just won't stop picking on you. That's when the wisest thing to do is to get out of there. After you run away, go straight to a grown-up and tell what happened. Let God and the grown-ups take care of the bully.

What Have We Learned?

- We *always* need to tell a grown-up when someone is bullying us.
- Sometimes we have to have courage and stand up to a bully.
- Sometimes we need our friends to help us with a bully.
- Sometimes a bully just needs is a friend.
- Sometimes we just have to run away from a bully.

Jesus loves bullies even though He doesn't like what they do. So when someone starts to bully you:

- First tell an adult. Then, pray and ask Jesus to help the bully—and you.
- Ask Jesus to help you to be full of courage.
- Ask Jesus to help you forgive the bully when he stops being a bully.
- Remember, don't let a bully make you sad.

How Parents Can Help

Today in America more than 160,000 children stay home from school every day because they are afraid of a bully! Most adults can still remember being bullied or seeing it happen to others. Child-to-child violence is becoming all too common in our schools—Christian or public.

It can happen in the earliest grades. That is why it is important for parents and kids to talk about what to do if they face a bully. *Big Bad Bible Bullies* is a fun, Bible-based way to discover how to respond.

Teachers and counselors, as well as parents, help kids learn safety strategies to use in different bullying situations. The Bible includes some really cool stories that show how to use these responses. Some of the most famous stories in the Bible give kids what they need to know to handle bullies the right way.

I pray that as you read these stories, the Holy Spirit will give you the wisdom and strength to live in the safety of good relationships with others. May God bless you with peace!

—Pastor Scott